Dislocative Disillusionment

(COMING SOON TO A CHISTIAN NEAR YOU?)

Rev. James DuJack

Printed in the United States of America

First Printing, 2012

ISBN: 0615697712
ISBN-13: 978-0615697710

Oakwood Covenant Press
260 Oakwood Avenue
Troy, NY 12182

Scripture Quotations are from The Holy Bible,
King James Version

DEDICATION

To Rev. Tom Clark, who through decades has
demonstrated faithful dedication and determination;
and whose friendship has been indispensible,
especially during my episodes of the common plight
described in these pages.

This booklet is the reworking of a sermon delivered to OBC on August 19, 2012, based on the Scriptural text of Isaiah 40:18-31.

CONTENTS

Introduction

INTRODUCTION

"Why sayest thou, O Jacob, and speakest, O Israel, My way is hid from the LORD, and my judgment is passed over from my God?" Isaiah 40:27

Our title this morning is Dislocative Disillusionment. It is a title with a subtitle. A question as a subtitle. "Coming soon to a Christian near you?"

Today we will address this most pertinent of issues, but we will also not fail to explore the Covenant Cure for Dislocative Disillusionment. What is Dislocative Disillusionment? Well, since everybody and their brother seems to be diagnosing a new disorder, I thought I would join the club! Perhaps we should call this syndrome "DD".

Perhaps it will rival similar commercials we have all seen on the T.V. I have no idea as to whether or not any official designation exists. I have not checked in with the American Medical Association or the National Psychiatric Society. Whether or not they would acknowledge this, I do not know. I do know, deep down in my bones and in my own soul, and with all kidding aside that the people of God can and have been afflicted with DD. I also know that the times are ripe for another outbreak; even an epidemic. Here in Isaiah 40:27 we see a symptomatic glimpse of DD.

"Why sayest thou, O Jacob, and speakest, O Israel, My way is hid from the LORD and my judgment is passed over from my God?" Isaiah 40:27

This is when the believer addresses God and charges: "that is not fair... **you are not fair.**" This is when a believer has become emotionally certain that they have not received a fair shake. They say things like, "I don't know where you are and you don't seem to care where I am"! They believe they have been wronged. The cry of their heart is "you promised more... you promised better."

This disorder therefore does concern believers. Not only can believers get this, on some levels they are really the only ones who can! The whole of this passage is about Isaiah ministering to those afflicted with it.

Moving very quickly let me sketch out seven aspects or angles at which we should view this passage.
1. Consistent closeout (all of Isaiah 40)
2. Context: Captivity (Exile in Babylon)
3. Contemporary Application
4. Common Plight (Psalm 73)
5. Creator and Continuing Ruler
6. Covenantal Cure
7. Chiastic Structure?

Now before we dive in, I suppose I ought to better define Dislocative Disillusionment. Disillusionment has to do with hopeful idealism losing out and being replaced by despair and bitterness. Dislocative modifies the type of disillusionment: owing to a new place. This is where it is asked "how did we, how did I get **here!!**"

CHAPTER 1:
CONSISTENT CLOSEOUT

Though our sermon text focused on verse 27 only, my purpose here is to show how the entire closeout section of Isaiah 40, (that is verses18-31) is consistent with the theme of the entirety of Isaiah 40. First of all, therefore, as is true of many Bible references, verses in Isaiah 40 are far too often plucked completely out of context. All of Isaiah 40 has addressed this theme of DD. Recalling previous sermons:

Isaiah 40:1-5, "Her Warfare is Accomplished", Isaiah has been ministering to the people of God concerning what is beyond the fall of Judah. He had been, as it were, ministering at the death bed of Judah.

In Isaiah 40:6-14, he reminded them of "The Sovereign, The Shepherd, and The Spirit", that indeed the trinity was at work in Judah's recovery.

In Isaiah 40:15-17, Isaiah reveals how God is in a class all his own, making the "Supreme Comparison". There he reveals that all nations are comparatively insignificant. Jehovah is to be worshipped; "Fire and Knife". Even Lebanon in all its glory is not sufficient, neither would be the sacrifice of all her beasts. As Isaiah 53:11 states, Jesus Christ is the satisfaction of God.[1]

---

[1] The fullness of Isaiah 53:11 is as follows: "He shall see the travail of his soul, and shall be satisfied; by his knowledge shall my righteous servant justify many; for he shall bear their iniquities." Nothing but Jesus satisfies God and God is satisfied. There are no more comforting words in the scripture!

Dislocative Disillusionment

CHAPTER 2:
CONTEXT: CAPTIVITY

All of these have been reminders to God's now conquered and exiled people of His continuing rule and purposes. The context therefore of this entire section not only textual, but historical, is that of the captivity. The people of God having been hauled away in chains, literally, having been death-marched into Babylon some 800 miles from home, mark this context. Don't forget that these were those that were not killed by the famine, the sword, and the pestilence which had visited upon Jerusalem. These "lucky ones" (not so surprisingly) fall victim to a great captivity temptation: **Dislocative Disillusionment**, i.e. "How did we get here?"

This was no mere "New Normal". It was not just uncomfortable. Remember Isaiah 28:20.

"For the bed is shorter than that a man can stretch himself on it: and the covering narrower than that he can wrap himself in it.

This is not merely that. It is not about the bed too short and the blanket too small. It is not just uncomfortable. This is far beyond that. This is a whole different place, literally and figuratively. This was a people swallowed up. This was a people finding themselves in the midst of a sea of paganism, a whole new world, a whole new culture. This was a people who at a minimum were going through an identity crisis.

CHAPTER 3:
CONTEMPORARY APPLICATIONS

What are the contemporary applications? We, for sure, have already entered the new normal. We have already experienced Isaiah 28:20... the bed too short, the blanket too small. Examples of this abound. We find them in every corner of contemporary culture. We are in the midst of a deep, steep, national decline and disintegration. Several previous sermons have made note of this. Our society is experiencing great discomfort. As I said, discomfort is one thing, dislocation is quite another.

Individuals have endured dislocations: divorced, bankruptcy, foreclosure. These are life changing events, where by you land in a whole different place. Maybe you've been fired. Maybe you are retired. Maybe you have experienced a disabling illness or injury. Maybe you have been a victim of the increasing crime and violence in our society. Corporately, our dislocations may or may not be literal, physically.... And I do not rule that out! But we certainly can be just as dislocated as the Israelites of old and subject to the same captivity temptation: Dislocative Disillusionment. This is where we experience a sense of loss of identity, of a people being swallowed up, surrounded in the midst of a pagan world and culture. You don't have to be a Michael Savage fan to know that borders, language, and culture are gone. [2]

Brothers and sisters, this transition is right before our

---

[2] Michael Savage is a bestselling author, and the voice of "the Savage Nation" radio program. Many of his most important and successful productions center on borders, language and culture.

eyes!   Already, I often wake up and look out at our societal landscape and say "How did we get here?" Often followed by, "Lord where are you?"

CHAPTER 4:
COMMON PLIGHT

Dislocative disillusionment, DD is a common plight. Job, like us, suffered from it. His cries in Job 23 reveal his symptoms. In addition, specifically in Job 27:2 and 34:5, he charges God with injustice.

"As God liveth, who hath taken away my judgment; and the Almighty, who hath vexed my soul." Job 27:2

"For Job hath said, I am righteous; and God hath taken away my judgment". Job 34:5

Jeremiah had an even more acute case.

"O Lord, thou hast deceived me, and I was deceived; thou art stronger than I, and hast prevailed. I am in derision daily, everyone mocketh me." Jeremiah 20:7

His internal conflict is even more extreme.

"Then I said, I will not make mention of him, nor speak any more in his name. But his word was in mine heart as a burning fire shut up in my bones, and I was weary with forbearing, and I could not stay." Jeremiah 20:9

In addition to these, the Psalmist provides a classic example and case of Dislocative Disillusionment. Let's look at Psalm 73. First we see that in verse 1, he is completely orthodox. He was able to talk a good game.

"Truly God is good to Israel, even to such as are of a clean heart." Psalm 73:1

Next and immediately, we notice that as for him it was a different story. Things were not working out. He was in a different place.

"But as for me, my feet were almost gone; my steps had well nigh slipped." Psalm 73:2

What is happening here is (as he explains over the course of the next ten verses) that the world seems upside down and completely backwards. The wicked prosper, the righteous man's cause is thwarted, etc., etc. He has a very bad case of DD.

In verse 13, he claims that whole his righteous motives and efforts have been for naught.

"Verily I have cleansed my heart in vain, and washed my hands in innocency." Psalm 73:13

He claims he doesn't want to talk about it.

"If I say, I will speak thus; behold, I should offend against the generation of thy children." Psalm 73:15

It is in fact so bad, that he doesn't even want to think about it.

"When I thought to know this, it was too painful for me." Psalm 73:16

Then we come to verse 17. Here everything changes. We come to the hinge; the Psalmist enters the presence of God.

*"**Until** I went into the sanctuary of God; **then** understood I their end." Psalm 73:17*

Here in the presence of God, the tabernacle of God, the worship of God, he gains his corrective lense. We will develop this more fully in the chapters ahead. For now, we should note that there is no more disillusionment. Now he sees clearly.

*"**Surely** thou didst set them in slippery places; thou castedst them down into destruction." Psalm 73:18*

A remarkable remediation is revealed in what follows:

"Thus my heart was grieved, and I was pricked in my reins. So foolish was I, and ignorant; I was as a beast before thee.

Nevertheless, I am continually with thee; thou hast holden me by my right hand. Thou shalt guide me with thy counsel and afterward receive me to glory. Whom have I in heaven but thee? And there is none upon earth that I desire beside thee. My flesh and my heart faileth; but God is the strength of my heart, and my portion forever.
Psalm 73: 21-26

The passage closes out with Covenant Renewal/Worship language as the Psalmist speaks of drawing near. [3]
"But it is good for me to draw near to God; I have put my trust in the Lord God, that I may declare all thy works." Psalm 73:28

That which he didn't want to think about or talk about, now he can't say enough.

---

[3] Drawing near, coming near, even near bringing are all "approach" aspects of worship. Rev. Jeff Meyer's seminal work "The Lord's Service" captures the essence of worship as established and outlined in Leviticus. Rev. Jim Jordan and Rev. Peter Liethart have also done ground-breaking work in the area of covenant renewal worship.

Dislocative Disillusionment

CHAPTER 5:
CREATOR AND CONTINUING RULER

While dislocative disillusionment is a common plight, a general remedy that virtually all commentators cite is how God reminds his people that he is creator and continuing ruler. You may be feeling dislocated but consider; not only is God very big but He has a very big tent. You may be somewhere that you have not been, but God is King over all places.

"It is he that sitteth upon the circle of the earth, and the inhabitants thereof are as grasshoppers; that stretcheth out the heavens as a curtain, and spreadeth them out as a tent to dwell in." Isaiah 40:22

God has a very big tent and all are under His continuing rule.
"That bringeth the princes to nothing; he maketh the judges of the earth as vanity." Isaiah 40:23

Look further at verse 28:
"Hast thou not known? Hast thou not heard, that the everlasting God, the Lord, the Creator of the ends of the earth, fainteth not, neither is weary? There is no searching of his understanding." Isaiah 40:28

In this, His universe, all is (continuing) under His dominion and control.
"Lift up your eyes on high, and behold who hath created these things, that bringeth out their host by number; he calleth them all by names by the greatness of his might, for that he is strong in power, not one faileth." Isaiah 40:26

As you can see, He names, He commands even the stars, and they obey! Therefore, as a baseline for recovery for DD we remember a verse like ....

"Being confident of this very thing, that he which hath begun a
good work in you will perform it until the day of Jesus Christ.:"
Philippians 1:6

CHAPTER 6:
COVENANTAL CURE

Brothers and sisters, more than a mere baseline for recovery, more than a general remedy, there is a cure for Dislocative Disillusionment. The cure is covenantal: Christ's Covenant. It is spiritual and it is structural. Isaiah in the whole of this passage ministers to his people with a spirit and a structure that is all too clear. When I first sat down and looked at this passage, I was sitting there just minding my own business. Then for reasons, and by means known only to God, I saw His Covenant. Don't miss this. It is really neat, but you will have to concentrate. Use the chart on the following pages or your own Bible. Place the last fourteen verses of Isaiah 40 side by side (18-24 and then 25-31), they will look like this.

Isaiah 40:18-24

18. To whom then will ye liken God? Or what likeness will ye compare unto him?

19. The workman melteth a graven image, and the goldsmith spreadeth it over with god, and casteth silver chains.

20. He that is so impoverished that he hath no oblation chooseth a tree that will not rot; he seeketh unto him a cunning workman to prepare a graven image, that shall not be moved.

21. Have ye not known? Have ye not heard? Hath it not been told you from the beginning? Have ye not understood from the foundations of the earth?

22. It is he that sitteth upon the circle of the earth, and the inhabitants thereof are as grasshoppers; that stretcheth out the heavens as a curtain, and spreadeth them out as a tent to dwell in:

23. That bringetht the princes to nothing; he maketh the judges of the earth as vanity.

24. Yea, they shall not be planted; yea, they shall not be sown: yea, their stock shall not take root in the earth: and he shall also blow upon them, and they shall wither, and the whirlwind shall take them away as stubble.

Isaiah 40:25-31

25. To whom then will ye liken me, or shall I be equal? Saith the Holy One.

26. Lift up your eyes on high, and behold who hath created these things, that bringeth out their host by number; he calleth them all by names by the greatness of his might, for that he is strong in power; not one faitheth.

27. Why sayest thou, O Jacob, and speakest, O Israel, My way is hid from the LORD, and my judgment is passed over from my God?

28. Hast thou not known? Hast thou not heard, that the everlasting God, the LORD, the Creator of the ends of the earth, fainteth not, neither is weary? There is no searching of his understanding.

29. He giveth power to the faint; and to them that have no might he increaseth strength.

30. Even the youths shall faint and be weary, and the young men shall utterly fall:

31. But they that wait upon the LORD shall renew their strength; they shall mount up with wings as eagles; they shall run, and not be weary; and they shall walk, and not faint.

Isaiah is here ministering to his people afflicted (knowingly or otherwise) with dislocative disillusionment. He here, shows them (knowingly or otherwise) the covenant. Looking back at the chart let's note two things:

1. There are two sets of seven verses.
2. There are two sets of five themes. These themes are as follows:
    a. God
    b. Man
    c. Law
    d. Consequences (or cause and effect)
    e. Future[4]

Verses 18 – 24 represent a covenant unto judgment, for worldlings. This is what God is doing, and how he is dealing with them; the Babylonian captors.

Verses 25 – 31 represent a covenant unto grace for His elect. This is what God is doing and how He is dealing with us. Though Judah is then in exile, this anticipates their return.

Let's look at some other details of this dual covenant. First we will note the impersonal nature of verses 18 – 24. From beginning to end, we see third person pronouns. This marks a drastic contrast to the personal nature of the personal pronouns and personal names listed in verses 25 – 31. Highlighting this contrast, note how in verses 18 God is simply referred to as God. That is "El" in the Hebrew. Compare that to verse 25, where God invokes a comparison to "me".

---

[4] These themes summarize the five point "THEOS" covenant model. "That You May Prosper" by Rev. Ray Sutton was a landmark achievement in covenantal analysis. Dr. Gary North has several volumes committed to the fleshing out of this model.

Note the following personal names:
Jacob – verse 27
Israel – verse 27
LORD (Jehovah) – verse 27
LORD (Jehovah) – verse 28
LORD (Jehovah) – verse 31

Here we see a threefold presentation of God, each in His covenant name.

There are other poignant contrasts. In 18 – 24, there is a looking at one's own works. In 25 – 31, there is a lifting up of the eyes unto the creation. Note Psalm 19:1.
"Indeed the heavens declare the glory of God and the firmament shows his handiwork."

Strikingly, verse 21 and 28 are expressions of what God has communicated. This is a reference to His Law/Word. This centerpiece highlights His revelation to mankind. Ironically, these two verses also hint toward an evolutionary versus creation contrast. Furthermore there is corresponding cause and effect. In verses 22 and 23, there are negative sanctions and judgment while the theme of verse 29 is about the positive blessings of grace. Verse 30 does not nullify this. It speaks to two things.
1. That this is not a work of the flesh.
2. That what is begun in the spirit cannot be fulfilled by the flesh as St. Paul affirms in Galatians 3:2-3
"This only would I learn of you, received ye the spirit by the works of the law, or by the hearing of faith? Are you so foolish? Having begun in the spirit, are ye now made perfect by the flesh?"

Each passage closes out concerning the future. Verse

24 speaks to the perished hope of the worldling, while verse 31 speaks to the great future promised for the child of God.

Set before the people of God we here see God working covenantally. First, "verses 18 – 24" a covenant unto judgment for the worldling: followed by "verses 25 - 31" a covenant unto grace for His elect. These beautiful verses that display God's covenantal cure are not disconnected from the horrific cultural context of a people with dislocative disillusionment.

CHAPTER 7:
CHIASTIC STRUCTURE?

As if that the covenantal structure seen earlier is not enough, and on the basis of our theology conference from last weekend[5], I now wonder if we might add a chiastic structure to the pattern Isaiah has set forth.

There can be no doubt that Isaiah is setting forth a rebuilding of Israel in this passage. A new world is coming into view. Rev. Jordan showed us how God rebuilds all things according to the pattern of the seven days of creation. These two sets of seven seem to follow suit. Do these operate chiastically? I'll have to leave to minds greater than mine if and how a possible double chiasm fully plays itself out in Isaiah 40:18 -31.

---

[5] Oakwood Bible Church, "Summer Theology Conference 2012" Rev. Jim Jordan, during his presentations, connected the chiastic dots for us. He showed us not only the chiastic structure of the days of creation, but also how this pattern is repeated in several key passages specifically as well as generally throughout the scriptures.

Dislocative Disillusionment

CHAPTER 8:
CONCLUSION

This sermon and this passage close out Isaiah 40. We have seen Isaiah doing a wonderful work of ministry here, for a people going into exile and in need of hope and assurance. As the context is that of captivity, these were those suffering acutely from dislocative disillusionment. Hopeful idealism had turned to despair and bitterness. We've also seen that this is a common plight. Not only have we referenced Job, Jeremiah, and the Psalmist, but Saints from every generation have endured trials and temptations of this sort. Thankfully there is not only a general remedy and a baseline for recovery. There is also a covenantal cure! Many of us have and/or may soon be facing not only the discomfort of a new normal but also the disillusionment that can accompany dislocation.

Brothers and sisters, if you or someone you know is suffering from dislocative disillusionment, show them the covenantal cure, and have them know that God creates and makes all things new.

Dislocative Disillusionment

www.ingramcontent.com/pod-product-compliance
Lightning Source LLC
Chambersburg PA
CBHW060600030426
42337CB00019B/3578